For my family and friends who helped me through the toughest season. Thank you, I love you.

For the opportunity of a lifetime at just the right time.

For anyone who has had their heart broken. I'm so sorry.

And of course

For you,

Before.

(I don't know you

now.)

NEW YORK

April [20], 2018

The saddest day

The day Love decided to go

And left me praying on the floor

Talking to myself or maybe God

"you're okay, you're okay

I knew I could describe sadness as a color now

  the blue of his eyes

As he looked at me

My heart in his hands (they were shaking)

He was trying to give it back to me

  as gently as he could

  "I'm so sorry"

You left me

so quickly

so completely

And then I left me

Our last kiss hurt

It makes sense really

Our lips chapped from crying for hours

A sandpaper goodbye

I walked from 190th to 28th street.

I asked the city to keep our memories.

With every step I felt our story saved

in the etchings of New York City.

I can let you go.

I am no longer afraid that no one will remember.

New York has saved the stories of many lovers,

So I know she is up to the task.

Between the lights of the GWB you can see

a snapshot of our dreams

and

if you walk from 42nd street

to the A train at Columbus Circle,

north along 9th Avenue,

after the shows let out,

you can still hear us laughing,

bundled under the snow.

I forgave Central Park for being a place where I loved you

I left a poem on the table

And I left New York City

MIAMI

I went to the ocean

The last time I saw her, you were here too

I wanted to give her my tears

To help give you away

She told me to keep them

She was salty enough anyway

You just forgot love

It's okay baby I
understand

Look through
my love letters in the
blue box next to my
bed

the ones you wrote
to me,

(the ones about each
room of the house

my favorites).

See how you
promised

a future together.

Remember the
details of our story.

If you can't find it
there baby

let me show you all
the pictures.

You hated me taking
so many

but this is why I did

so you would never
forget

the millions of
moments

the little things

the big things

that shaped the last
six years.

Can you show me the
letters too?'

Baby where did you go?

I'm here

I'm here

I can't even write good poems.
All I can think of is
     I miss you
        I miss you
           I miss you
              I miss you
                 I miss you

Sadness still wakes me in the morning

though now she whispers more gently

she takes my hand

lays down in the bed

and lets me know she is going to stay for awhile

I can't call you my ex-boyfriend yet

That's not the right word

You can't be the ex of anything

When you are still my whole life

What's the word love?

You're the writer,

Can't you even give me this:

What's the word for

"The man I love who is lost"

  (I love you)

I will love you through this

Please do everything you can to find yourself

Can you find the boy

with the messy hair and the blue eyes?

Can you tell him I love him, please?

Don't be anxious baby

I'm lost too

2 MONTHS

You are still everywhere

I am getting used to the lack of you

(I hate both)

You said you were "keeping things quiet"

(I hate that)

That's not fair

My life since you left has been

high volume

grief

and change

and deep loud noisy loss

3 MONTHS

It's been long enough now

hasn't it?

I think of you less

Please don't be mad

I'm trying to equally

love you and let you go

You asked me to

THE AIRPORT

I think the first thing I would tell her
would be that sometime
(sooner than she'd think)
Happiness will run back into her life
will take her by the hands laughing as She says
"Oh it is good to see you old friend. Show Me what
you've learned."

LONDON

I walked alone

No music

No podcasts

Or phone calls

Or anyone by my side

I walked these streets where I had been before

I swear they remembered me

Peaceful and lovely

Watercolor buildings, English in their stoic beauty

Portobello Market packed with trinkets

Each cobblestone hewn with history

Each step a journey back to gratitude

I walked and tried to memorize

the way London smelled

like caramel, the hard candy kind

that my Papa used to keep in his pockets

He'd hand me one, just to make me smile.

And I realized, if I had to explain,

this is what London has always meant to me

that feeling of a random act of kindness

Inspiration for joy

Five years ago on this street

it filled my soul with that same sweetness

as spontaneous as the candy you didn't expect to have before dinner

I try to remember the feeling

I keep walking

I put gratitude in my pocket for later

I am both sad and grateful in so many ways

4 MONTHS

I asked God again
"can it still be him?

BERGEN, NORWAY

I was sad in the fjords of Norway

It was the perfect place.

Melancholy mountains with

deep green, massive faces, huge

laugh lines down the front.

Or maybe they are creases carved

 from one big tear from God

That feels familiar to me

Tears carve paths down my cheeks too

Sadness and water are two things that can change
a landscape.

I wondered

if I could swim to shore

walk the tiny zig zag street

into the clouds

where there might be a good place

quiet and misty

to say out loud

"I miss you"

I bet this mountain knows how to keep a secret

BARCELONA AND VILLEFRANCHE (OR MEDICINE)

I do a lot of wandering and shopping

people watching and gelato eating

I pet as many dogs as I see

I try on silly hats

I take too many selfies

I say "hello" in the new language of the day

I make a mental note of how the air smells

If Barcelona was a candle it would be "Mandarin Rain"

Villefranche would be "Espresso and Suntan Lotion"

I stand in the rain when it falls

in the sun when it shines

I let the wind blow new languages and music through my hair

I take steps up the winding side streets

If there is a wedding proceeding into the cathedral

Or a protest in the square, I watch

I thank God for the way it all makes me feel very
alive

I smile too much

I buy a postcard

I decide I'd like to stay a little longer

CORSICA

She told me the seashell necklace would bring
happiness and good fortune

I prayed that it might work

NORWAY 2, 3, AND 4

The earth in Geiranjerfjord

looks like a heart

that has been broken right down the middle

and yet

it is the most beautiful thing

I have ever seen

I promise if everyone could take a field trip to the top of Mt Floyen

We would have world peace

There is no way anyone could want to fight after they had seen the view

They would feel very small amongst the glacier carved mountains

They would hear the waterfalls, see the way the pale-yellow sunlight stretches for decades

I think there is so much hatred in the world

Because so many people have not even glimpsed

the *real world – God's world.*

Come to Norway, let me take you

 in a cable car to the top of the fjord.

I'll buy you a soft serve ice cream

sprinkled with rainbows

and I will show you what I mean

"What word would you use to describe it here?"

"Magic" she said

I agreed

Alone in my kayak

Alone in my world

Rocks and raindrops

Cold water and warm tears

There was a release

taking off a brand I had been wearing this year

When sadness happens, we wear it

Like a label on the forehead

so I didn't have to explain

this love MEANT something

Here is my sadness to prove it

I set my paddle down

I was not alone

Dozens of purple jelly fish surrounded me

Checking in, they heard that I was free

The waterfalls rushed down to meet me

They wanted to let me know they were proud of me

I had made it here

The muscles in my arms had pushed me to greet
them

The muscle in my chest had never once accepted
the word "broken"

The breeze sang through my lungs; she was
cleaning out the last bits

Reminding me when I said "I can't even breathe"

Now I can

I looked around at the massive scale of the
physical world around me

I would never be too much here

It would be impossible to be

 "too emotional"

"too excited",

 to give "too much"

There was such comfort in that

In being very little

In finding new things to love

Like kayaking

Like noticing faces in the rocks

Like singing "Amazing Grace" to the angels in the
fjord

Like freedom

"yes, magic"

"that's perfect."

GIBRALTAR

I just wanted you to know that I saw the coast of
Africa today,

saw the sun set on the water

And I loved you all over again

Thank you for shaping my life

I still desperately wish you were in it

I hope you felt a bit of my love tonight

All the way from Gibraltar, Spain

VIGO

I run now

I used to hate running

Now I love the way it gives my energy somewhere to go

It lets the thoughts run too

But I can run faster than them now

I have been conditioning

I run somewhere between the ocean and the shore

Comfortable in the in-between places of life

That's a lot of what being twenty five is

I am in-between answers

I am in-between decades

I am in-between countries on this journey through the world

I am never in one place, neither are my dreams, neither is my heart

I am growing and changing and grieving and healing and running

And I am learning

That there is happiness in the in-between

If you don't believe me

Come feel the way my heart beats

I am running on the beach in Vigo!

I have no answers, I have a long way to go

but I have velvet sparkled sand under my toes

I leave footprints, the waves take them back for keeps

There is enough joy here, I try to catch it

OCEAN

I lied

I said I wouldn't write about you anymore

But you mean more to me than final answers

there are more words between the lines

That's the thing about us isn't it?

We are between answers

I found you in the space between yes and no

Which makes sense

That's where hearts get left after they are broken

The purgatory where souls wait after they are

separated

 from the one they thought was theirs

Before they are free to find another

to make coffee with, to dance with, to share

We are the space between my fingers where you fit

The space between the frets on my guitar

How my lips feel between your freckles (the

constellation on your chest)

We only exist in those places

We fill each other up between what was and what

will be

That's why it is hard to choose words for you -

What comes after friendship and before love?

I haven't lived that in so long

I don't know how not to take you in all at once

How do I not pour myself into all your cracks until you overflow

or until we drown?

What would be the poem for us?

No wonder there is no answer

We are like ghosts

"You won't let me say no and I won't let me say yes"

LA PALMA/ MEDERIA (OR LESSONS OVER 2 DAYS, 2 CITIES, AND 3 COFFEES)

Remember your worth

Remember the words they gave you

Brave

Lovely

Strong

Remember there is someone who will want to look after you

But look after yourself first

It has not been long enough

There are still bits of you scattered around

Pages in your story book are all out of order

Take the time

Don't rush, only the hours can sort it

Just sit here

Read through each of the pages

Look at the black sand on the beach

Listen to the friends that have stayed

Smell the espresso waiting for you

Feel the sun planting kisses on your neck

Enjoy time to build again

LISBON

Let's begin again

Let's believe in
friendship

CADIZ

I like to think that God made the trams in Cadiz
yellow

Just because he knew I'd be visiting today

That he wanted signs rolling up and down every
street to say

I love you I love you I love you

I'm so glad you're here.

BARCELONA

To be a flower
in Barcelona!

To lay in the
window box

watching the stylish ladies
go by

They would
notice you are
beautiful

You would laugh

You
thought the
same about
them

5 MONTHS

Today I decided it was time to be grateful again

LANZAROTE

"Did you know Lanzarote is where people come to
get space?"
The tour guide asked us
Space from what?
I knew the answer
Space from it all
From all the things that make us feel very tied to
our cities,
our pain, our bank accounts, our soy lattes
It makes sense
We get ourselves so worked up
that we need to mount a camel
to go to the end of a volcano
to find space from it all.
Lanzarote looks like outer space
In so many ways it is the perfect choice
It has been here millions of years
These three hundred volcanos are much older
than your latest boy drama
than your anxiety about work
than your loneliness
than the time you spent in line at Starbucks
Three quarters of the island is covered in volcanic
ash
It is something violent and dangerous and
eruptive and unpredictable
yet it is called the valley of tranquility
People come to a place of destruction to find peace

I thought they were opposites
Maybe sometimes there has to be unpredictable
chaos
Black ash that covers what you thought you
recognized
Before there can be growth
The farmers of Lanzarote have been called
"Magicians of the Earth"
There is a strange beauty here
I think God is a magician too
"And now we are entering the Valley of Tranquility."

BRUGES, PARIS, ROTTERDAM, AND NORWAY

I have been looking for you, God

You said "Seek me" and so I sought

I have looked in my guilt, sure I would find you
there

With "not to dos" and rules

I had searched in my worries, confident you were
leading

the march of my anxieties

Saying over and over to do more, pray more,

not enough not enough not enough...

I have sought you in places

All over the world

Churches in Bruges, towers in Paris, statues in
Rotterdam

I found you in none of these places

You found me everywhere else

In my joy, you were there, waiting to celebrate
with me

As thrilled as I was

to try a fresh waffle

to hike through the trees

to sing at the piano

You found me in my gratitude

Weeping with the weeping willow tree,

common in our reverence for the beauty of the
park

counting the ducks by the pond

counting my blessings

You found me in the silly things

the perfect boots on sale

the friendly calls of "bonjour mademoiselle"

the smiles when I attempted my French.

You found me in the middle of a fjord

Sending sweet cold air through my lungs like
water after a day running in the sun

You showed me your face in the rocks, you said
"you are okay now, sit with me here"

You never left, you were always with me

Present in the millions of simple joys

Headlining in the amazing sights of the world

Not holding back or having time for subtleties
when it came to sunsets on the ocean

Always rooting for my happiness, always singing peace

You just wanted me to notice

And to trust a little more

"be still and know that I am God"

PARIS

I didn't write a poem in Paris

I didn't have time for writing, I was in Paris!

I had only five hours

and a lot of broken hope

I saw the Eiffel Tower

I had a coffee and ran down the Champs Elyses

I fell in love with

the way the buildings all wore the same uniform

the way the light spilled out of the flowerboxes

the way the gelato man said "oui"

and then I missed the train home

6 MONTHS

(NOT EXACTLY TO THE DAY)

How's New
York?

How's our
apartment?

When I think
of home

That's what I
still picture.

(You let me down.)

SOUTHHAMPTON

When the seasons change

Do you think "this is my first Fall without her"?

Do you notice the yellow leaves on the trees more
than the other colors?

Fall is hard for me

-that makes sense, it is when we fell in love

You have a hold on November

(and the rest of the year too)

But I was just wondering

as I have each day for months,

have you thought of me today?

AMSTERDAM (THE ONE WE DIDN'T GO TO)

This one is for all the places we didn't go

For the years we won't spend together

The couch we never agreed on,

The music that won't play in the kitchen.

I have written many poems to preserve the places we did go,

Even more about the places I have been since you left

But there haven't been any about what we don't get to do

About the life I don't get to share with you

The spot next to you on the airplane

The cab to our hotel, the nap on the bed before dinner,

The first time we would walk into Amsterdam

And I could say "look baby, we made it"

AMSTERDAM (THE ONE I WENT TO)

There is a bridge in Amsterdam
called "Love Lock Bridge"

It is so weighed down by the hundreds of
locks hanging on its' sides

That it had to be reinforced

There is still so much love
in the world

In Amsterdam, if you watch
the sun set on the canals

You can see it,

just watch out for the
bicycles.

THE CROSSING

The crossing from the Mediterranean to the
Caribbean felt symbolic

But I wasn't in the mood for poetry

I just wanted to be held

THE CARIBBEAN

I'm doing a lot of telling myself I'm beautiful

I'm praying a lot for freedom from guys who don't
make me feel lovely

I'm reminding myself every day that I am doing
the best that I can

There is still more ocean to sail.

COZUMEL

There are no poems in Mexico for me

I'm not sure why

There are margaritas

The people are fun and vibrant

There is music and men are selling tiny yellow
guitars on the streets

(I bought one)

There is so much joy

but I'm tired of the sunshine

of the way it keeps asking me to be grateful

I need a break from the adventure of it all

How selfish

I'm on a beach in Mexico with sun on my chest and
the ocean asking me to dance

And all I want is to be walking down a dark snowy
street in New York City

  (with you)

I need more time to be sad

9 MONTHS

Sometimes to fall asleep at night

I pretend I am back in New York City

I imagine that you have texted me

Don't wait up

the trains are bad tonight

I love you

sweet dreams gorgeous

It sounds crazy

It probably isn't useful for healing

Or taking steps on this big journey away from you

But I have to be honest

It helps me sleep

You're not here

But you're on your way home

The trains are just late in Brooklyn

JAMAICA

Almost 10 months "if you see him tell him I'm okay, okay?"

11 MONTHS

for months now I have been trying to find the right
end to the sentence "I miss you like..."

 Today I thought maybe

I miss you like a bird misses her wings

But it's more like the footless bird

Val talks of in *Orpheus Descending*

It has to remain forever in the wind

Yes

I miss you like the bird misses her feet.

Flying has never been the problem

 just without you

I have nowhere to land.

COSTA MAYA

Today the ocean invited me to dance

I'm so glad I said yes

She moved my hips in a way you never could

GRAND CAYMAN

I let the ocean lift me up

these days

I let people

lift me up too

ALL AROUND THE WORLD

There have been a lot of poems about the men

The ones that left, the ones that came after

But what about the women?

The ones who marched into the heartbreak

Armed with comfort, tea, wisdom, tissues and poems

The ones who met you where you were

(even on the floor)

who sat who listened who picked you up

who each found a piece of your heart

and worked together to puzzle it back

 to something you recognize as yourself

the ones who built a flower covered shield around
your heart,

stood at the entry way defending you against the men
who came next

the ones who knew you still needed time to heal

These are the women who shaped you

 The women who showed you

 It was time to

 fall back in love

 with *life*.

Keep living. Keep honoring yourself. And be ready with tea and tissues when it's their turn to be sad.

I YEAR.

1 YEAR AND TWO DAYS

I'm afraid of going back home

and not having the ocean

to run to

when I get very sad

I'm not sure the concrete buildings

will bring the same

peace

as salt water

in my hair

FALMOUTH

I'm grateful

I'm hopeful

I miss you

I look at the stars with someone new

he's not the "one"

he doesn't erase you

he doesn't replace you

he does remind me of you

great at conversation

the way he wants to know more

asks, then follows up

with a really good story

and a joke

I loved talking with you

I'll keep looking for that

it's not him,

it's not you,

but it's nice to remember

there will be others

who would love to share

 a meal

a movie

a story

a constellation

and just cross lives for a bit

no six year promise

no apartment lease

maybe even no kisses

for now I'm just

looking for someone

who I love to talk to

for now just

peanut butter M&Ms

and Ursa Minor

is enough

I'm grateful

I'm hopeful

(I miss you)

LABADEE

I am more gorgeous

than I have ever been

I have trapped enough

sunshine in my skin

to bring it back

and share it with anyone

who's feeling

cold

I've got rays to spare

FORT LAUDERDALE

thank you for being

the lightning bolt

to my heart

you were bright and electric

even though you were only

      a flash of light

           you shocked me

              back to life

NEW YORK

April 20, 2019

The lesson? The love will always stay. And that's
okay.

I got on the plane back to New York City.

EPILOGUE

Sometimes when we lose what we love, we find ourselves in places we never thought we'd go.

But that's where miracles are made: in the growing years. In the red lipstick and the "yes" to dinner. In the first note of the overture. In the postcard home. In the freckles on his nose. In the new start with a new script. In the salt water.

In the promise that the sun rises the same way on the ocean as it does in Amsterdam as it does in New York City.

Take your heartbreak and make something beautiful.

I did. And I will.

There have been mistakes, way too many tears, and lots of unfinished poems. There will be more. I am not afraid. I found I like traveling now.

I wonder where I will go next.

Bring on the rest of the journey.

69317819R00046

Made in the USA
Middletown, DE
20 September 2019